The Many Kinds of Big

by Dale-Marie Bryan

amicus readers

Ideas for Parents and Teachers

Amicus Readers let children practice reading informational texts at the earliest reading levels. Familiar words and concepts with close photo-text matches support early readers.

Before Reading

- Discuss the cover photo with the child. What does it tell him?
- Ask the child to predict what she will learn in the book.

Read the Book

- "Walk" through the book and look at the photos. Let the child ask questions.
- Read the book to the child, or have the child read independently.

After Reading

- Use the picture glossary at the end of the book to review the text.
- Prompt the child to make connections. Ask: What are other words for big?

Amicus Readers are published by Amicus
P.O. Box 1329, Mankato, MN 56002
www.amicuspublishing.us

Library of Congress
Cataloging-in-Publication Data
Bryan, Dale-Marie, 1953-
  The many kinds of big / Dale-Marie Bryan.
    page cm. -- (So many synonyms)
  ISBN 978-1-60753-506-5 (hardcover) -- ISBN 978-1-60753-536-2 (eBook)
  1. English language--Synonyms and antonyms--Juvenile literature. I. Title.
  aPE1591 .B755 2013
  428.1--dc23
                    2013006871

Photo Credits: David Ashley/Shutterstock Images, cover; Jim Agronick/Shutterstock Images, 1; Shutterstock Images, 3; Trevor Allen/Shutterstock Images, 4, 16 (top left); Ethan Daniels/Shutterstock Images, 7, 16 (middle left); Chris Dascher/iStockphoto, 8, 9, 16 (bottom left); Thinkstock, 10, 11, 16 (top right); Dale Walsh/iStockphoto, 13, 16 (middle right); Shutterstock Images, 14, 16 (bottom right)

Produced for Amicus by The Peterson Publishing Company and Red Line Editorial.

Editor Jenna Gleisner
Designer Becky Daum
Printed in the United States of America
Mankato, MN
July, 2013
PA 1938
10 9 8 7 6 5 4 3 2 1

What do you see that is big? Do you know other words that mean big? Words with similar meanings are synonyms.

4

Large means big.

Lobsters have two large claws that pinch. One claw is larger than the other. It is used to break apart food.

Huge means big.

Giant clams are huge. They live and grow in one spot their whole lives.

7

Gigantic means big.

Great white sharks are gigantic. Their mouths can fit 300 teeth!

Massive means big.

Orca whales are massive. They hunt in large groups called pods.

Enormous means big.

Humpback whales are enormous. They use their big tail fins to swim fast and jump out of the water.

13

Vast means big.

Oceans are vast. They are large enough to fit all of the big animals in the ocean.

Synonyms for Big

large
great in size

massive
very big and heavy

huge
very large

enormous
extremely big

gigantic
huge in size

vast
very large and
far reaching